Jesus Is for Kids

JESUS vs.
THE BAD GUYS

illustrated by DANIEL DUNCAN

written by CONNOR SHRAM
& JARED NEUSCH

Tyndale House Publishers
Carol Stream, Illinois

To our kids:

Clayton, Roey, Isla, and Avai, Grace, Adeline—
may you always know the God who looks like Jesus.

Visit Tyndale's website for kids at tyndale.com/kids.

Tyndale is a registered trademark of Tyndale House Ministries. The Tyndale Kids logo is a trademark of Tyndale House Ministries.

Jesus vs. the Bad Guys

Published in association with Pape Commons: a gathering of voices, www.papecommons.com

For manufacturing information regarding this product, please call 1-855-277-9400.

For information about special discounts for bulk purchases, please contact Tyndale House Publishers at csresponse@tyndale.com, or call 1-855-277-9400.

Library of Congress Cataloging-in-Publication Data

A catalog record for this book is available from the Library of Congress.

ISBN 978-1-4964-7816-0

Printed in China

30	29	28	27	26	25	24
7	6	5	4	3	2	1

A Note for Parents

Hi! We're Connor and Jared—authors and lifelong friends. Along with our wives, we are trying our best to raise our kids in the way of Jesus. We think kids learn best through imagination, and we both love to write and tell stories. We developed this series, Jesus Is for Kids, because the Gospels show us that children have always been drawn to Jesus. We want to present Jesus in a fun and playful way—all with the broader goal of helping kids explore the *meaning* behind Jesus' life and teachings in a way they'll understand. We wrote *this* book, *Jesus vs. the Bad Guys*, because we wanted to explore with our kids how Jesus overcomes evil. Does He beat up the bad guys like superheroes do? Does He ride in on a T. rex to stop them? Or does He defeat the bad guys through love and forgiveness? With all the struggles kids experience at school—and everything they hear about evil occurring around the world—we think it's important for kids to learn how Jesus teaches us to love our enemies, even from the earliest ages. Thanks for joining us on the journey!

Do you know who the *bad guys* are?

In Jesus' day, most people thought they knew who the bad guys were. They were the *Roman soldiers*. These guys were big meanies. They would take over other countries and steal all their money!

They would force some people to become *slaves*. They would hurt people. They would force strangers to carry their bags.

Before Jesus came, everyone hoped a new king would arrive and *do something* about these bad guys.

Once Jesus showed up, many people got excited. If Jesus became King, they thought they knew what His mission would be.

They imagined He was going to make all the bad guys pay.

It said so in one of their sacred scrolls! They called that day—the day they would all fight the bad guys—the Day of Revenge.

Sounds pretty cool, right? All the new King had to do was get up and say, "It's payback time!"

And one day, Jesus stood up in their meeting place and opened that very scroll.

The people all waited anxiously as Jesus started to read.

"I'm here to announce My new Kingdom!" Jesus declared. "I'm here to tell people about God's *favor* . . ."

Everyone held their breath. The very next line was about the Day of Revenge! They would *finally* get revenge on the big meanies.

But . . . Jesus just stopped reading. He rolled up the scroll and sat back down. He chose to leave out the part where the bad guys get beaten up.

A King who didn't want revenge on the bad guys? *What kind of King is that?*
The crowd got so mad at all the things Jesus said, they ran Him out of town.

Have you ever had to face any bad guys or bullies?
What did you do?
   They can be mean, and they can be scary.
And they can do all sorts of horrible things.
   What can anybody do?

One day, two of Jesus' friends had a big idea about how to fight some bullies. They said, "Just say the word, Jesus! God will give us the power to *shoot fireballs* at those bad guys!"

That would teach them.

But Jesus said *no*. He wanted to do things a different way.

But the bad guys were getting even worse.

They *hated* Jesus. They even wanted to *kill* Him. The disciples were getting nervous.
If Jesus wasn't going to fight the bad guys, how would they ever be *free*?

Another time, Jesus sat down with His friends on a hillside and told them what He wanted them to do.

"Don't fight evil with evil," Jesus said. "If someone hits you in the face, don't hit them back. If someone steals your shirt, offer them your coat too!"

Jesus' friends were shocked. How would they protect themselves?
The Roman meanies were everywhere!
   "And if those big Roman bad guys make you carry their stuff
for a mile? Well, carry their stuff for *two*."

That didn't make *any* sense. They wanted to *punch* and *kick* the bad guys. They wanted to throw their stupid stuff right back in their big smug faces! But Jesus didn't want them to do that. Instead, He said,

"I want you to love your enemies."

12

LOVE? The BAD GUYS?

But, Jesus, we can't love the bad guys! Then *nobody will stop them*. They'll keep stealing our lunch! They'll keep taking our clothes! They'll keep hurting us!

And they might even TRY TO KILL US!

You want us to *love* people like *that*?

One day, an angry mob showed up to arrest Jesus. The bad guys thought they had figured out how to stop Jesus from becoming King. They showed up with swords and clubs and spears, ready for a fight.

How would Jesus defeat the bad guys?

Remember: Jesus is *powerful.*
He is God's son. He healed the sick!
He walked on water!

HE STOPPED STORMS WITH HIS VOICE!

He even *raised a little girl from the dead.*

Jesus could be the *ultimate superhero.*
He could fight however He wanted—and
He would win no matter what.
    Jesus could have sent a

HURRICANE OF SHARKS

to eat all the bad guys.

Jesus could have made a FART CANNON that would shoot stink bombs so nasty, it would knock them out in three seconds flat.

BRRRAAAAPPP!!!

Jesus could have shot LASERS out of His eyes. Or He could have called down big, beefy ANGELS!

They were *waiting up in heaven for their King's command.*

But what did Jesus do?
He just let them tie Him up.

The bad guys were *winning*! Jesus' friend Peter was *not* cool with this.

He grabbed a sword and leaped into action! He ran at the bad guy who grabbed Jesus. He *swung with all his might . . .*

. . . and he cut off the bad guy's ear.

"NO!" Jesus shouted, stepping in the way.

"That isn't how we win, Peter," Jesus said. And then, reaching down, He picked up the bad guy's ear, and . . .

. . . *put his ear back on.*

Jesus' friends all ran away. They were scared for their lives, of course. And the bad guys meant business. They wanted to *kill* Jesus . . . and He didn't plan on stopping them.

Jesus was going to *love* the bad guys, even if they *killed* Him.

The soldiers put Jesus up on a cross. It was torture.

People shouted at Jesus while he was dying. Some were mocking, and others were desperate.

"If you really are the King, why aren't you fighting? And where are your big, beefy angels?"

"WHY DON'T YOU FIGHT BACK?!"

But then, just as Jesus was about to die, He *said* something.

It was His *secret weapon.*

It was the one and only thing that could ever possibly defeat all the bad guys. He said . . .

You see, Jesus knew something that we forget. The bad guys don't always think they're the bad guys! The bad guys *don't always know what they're doing*.

They do mean, horrible things because *they've lost sight of who they are*.

And only love can open their eyes.

If you punch them, they punch back.

If you kick them, they kick back even harder.

But if you *forgive them*?

Well, forgiveness
helps them see. It creates a road
back that anyone can take.
The Roman soldier who was
in charge of killing Jesus—the
big bad guy who took His life away—
even *he* realized the truth.
When he looked up at Jesus, he said,
"This really was the Son of God."

Jesus didn't *stay* dead. He rose again!

And guess what? *He still didn't take revenge.* He really did forgive the bad guys who had killed Him.

Jesus proved that *forgiveness* is more powerful than punches and kicks. And in the end, *love* wins over hate.

He could have *destroyed* the big, bad Romans! He could have taken over the world while riding a pet T. rex.

And the bad guys would be *so scared*, right? But that's the craziest thing: Jesus doesn't see people as good guys and bad guys. He sees everyone as worthy of love.

Today, followers of Jesus all over the world get His help to fight in the *exact same way* Jesus did.

They don't use fireballs or fart cannons. They don't just wait for a day of revenge. They do stand up against injustice—and when they're bullied, they *ask someone they trust for help.*

But they don't fight evil with evil. Instead, they fight evil with *love and forgiveness.* Sometimes, this means they get hurt. Sometimes, this means they *lose.* Sometimes, they have to create space because some people are unsafe. But they know their King Jesus will make things right one day. And they know the one and only secret weapon to stop evil, once and for all: